Draw Anything : Pencil Drawings Step By Step

Pencil Drawing Ideas for Absolute Beginners

By Gala Publication

Published By:

Gala Publication

ISBN-13: 978-1515200857
ISBN-10: 151520085X

©Copyright 2015 – Gala Publication

Table of Contents

Apple

Step 1

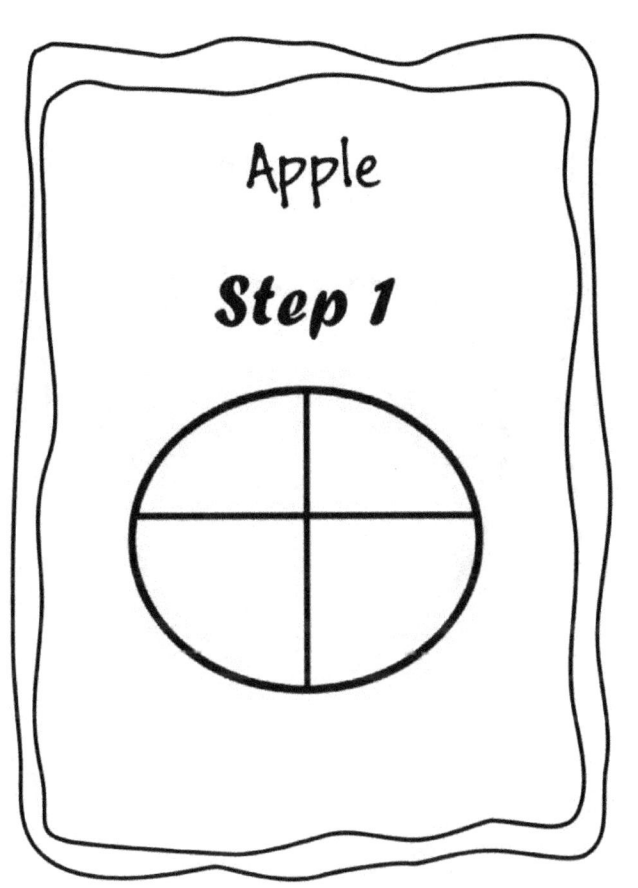

Step 2

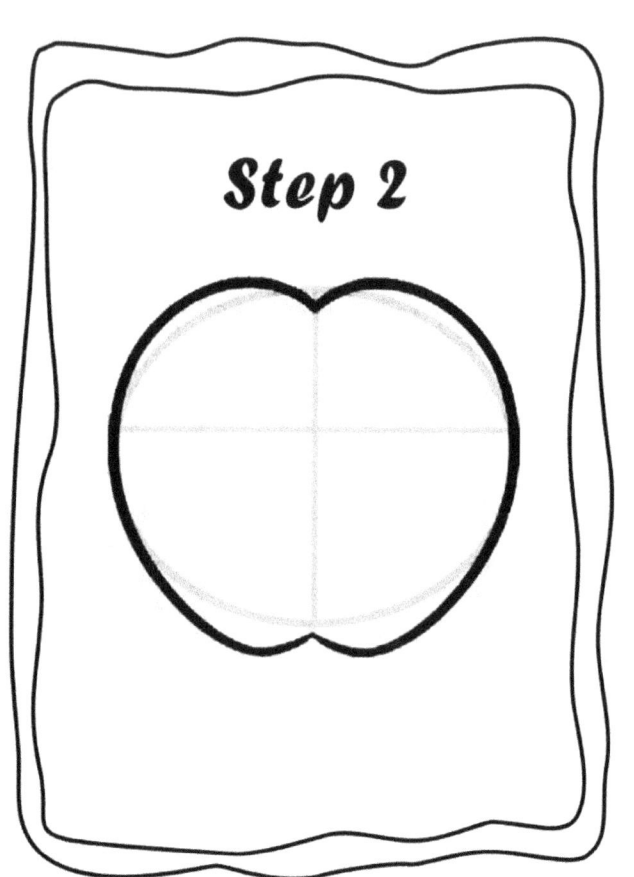

Step 3

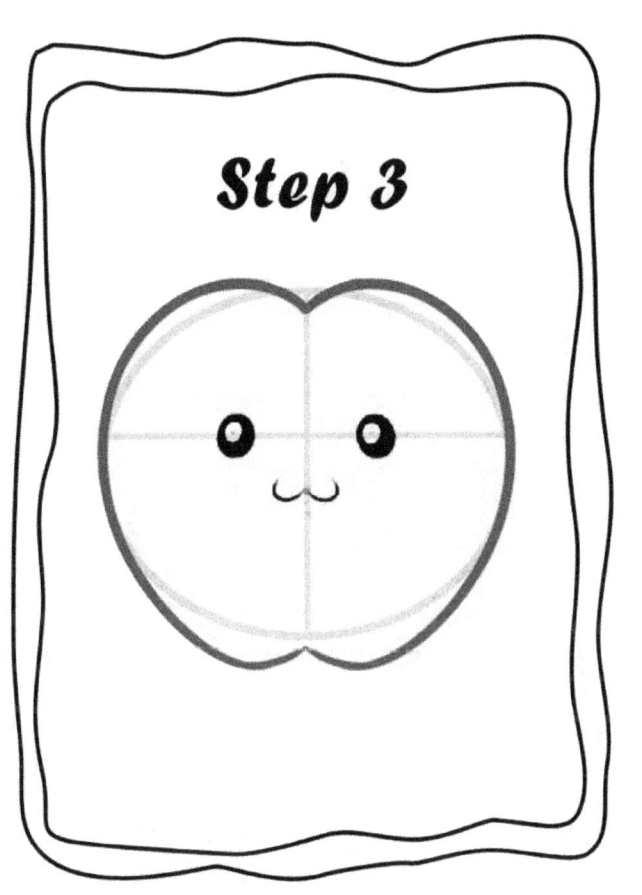

Step 4

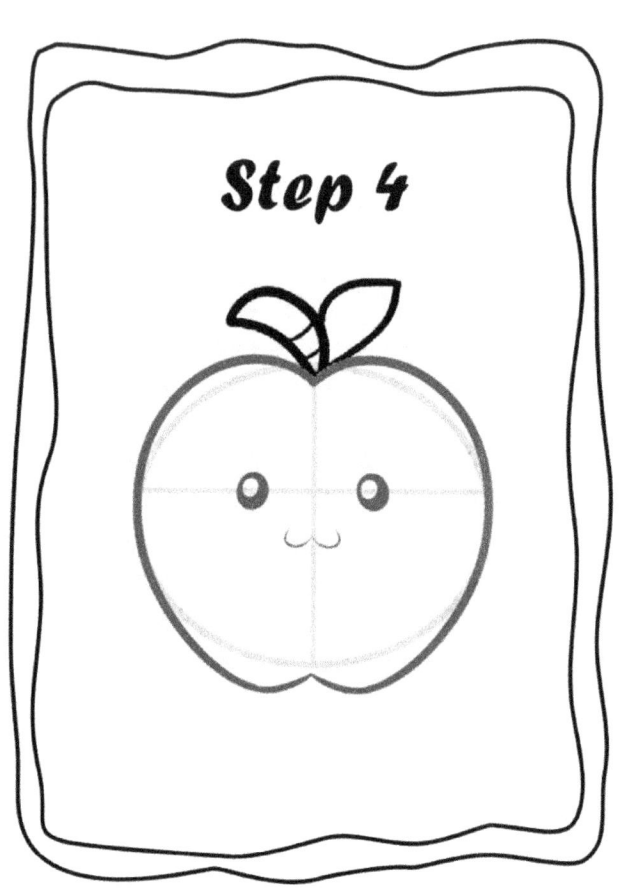

Step 5

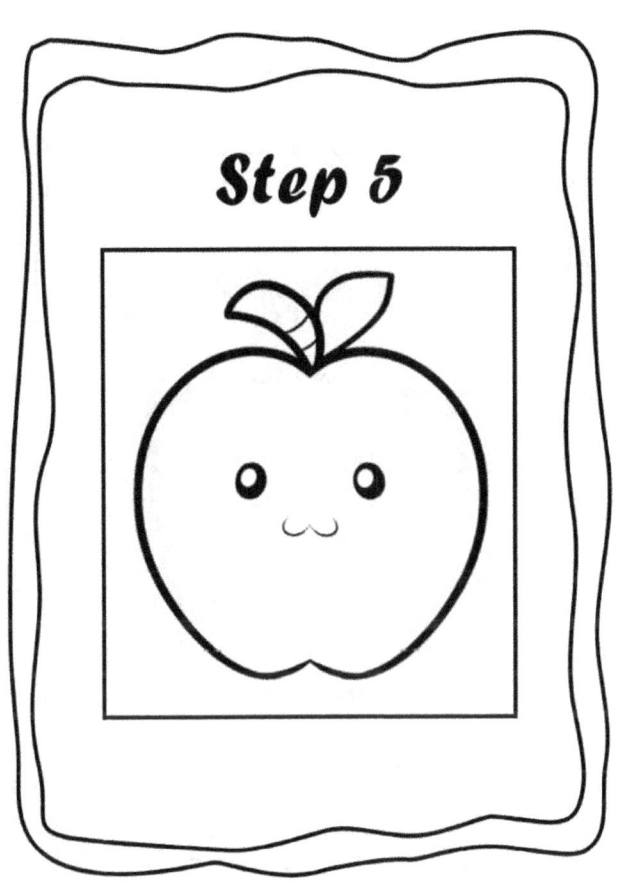

Drums

Step 1

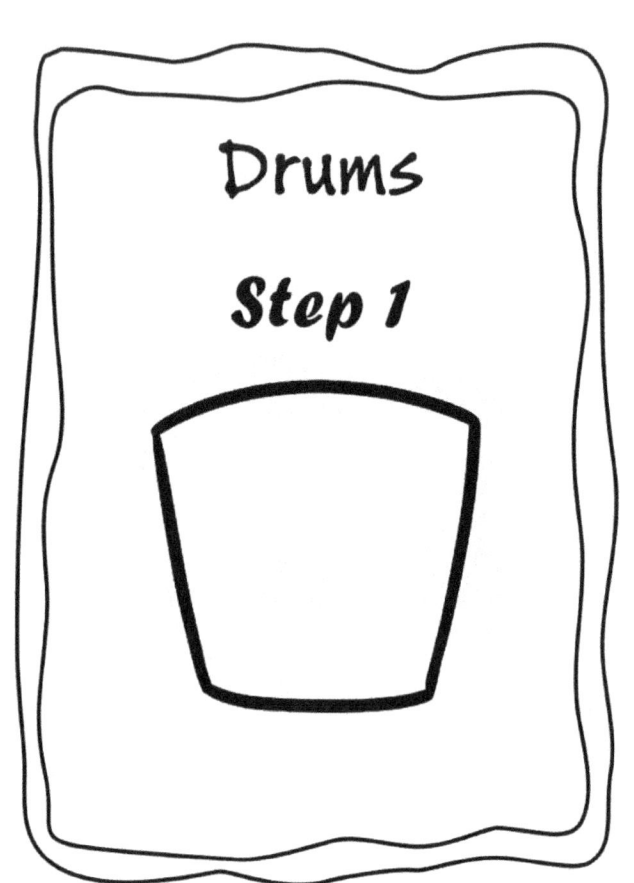

Step 2

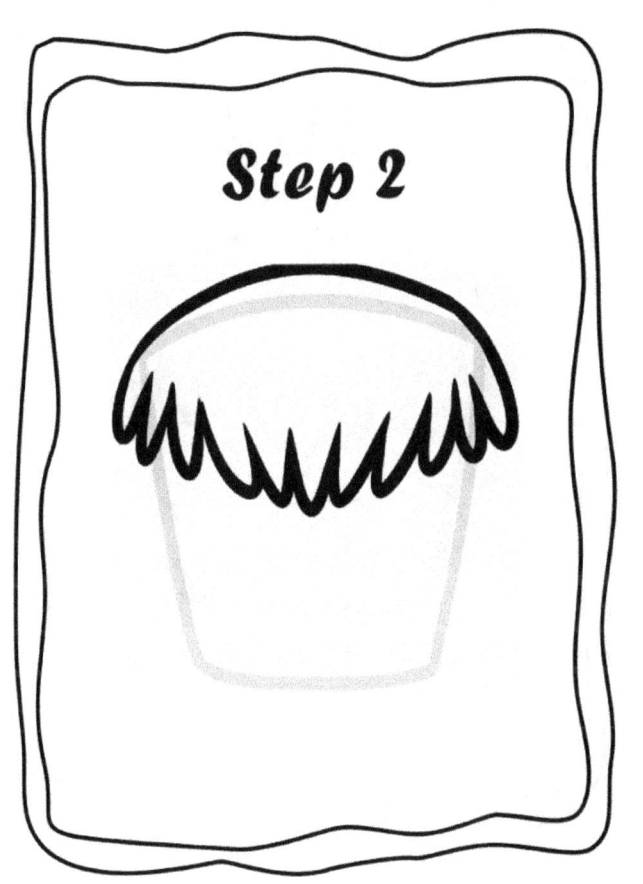

Step 3

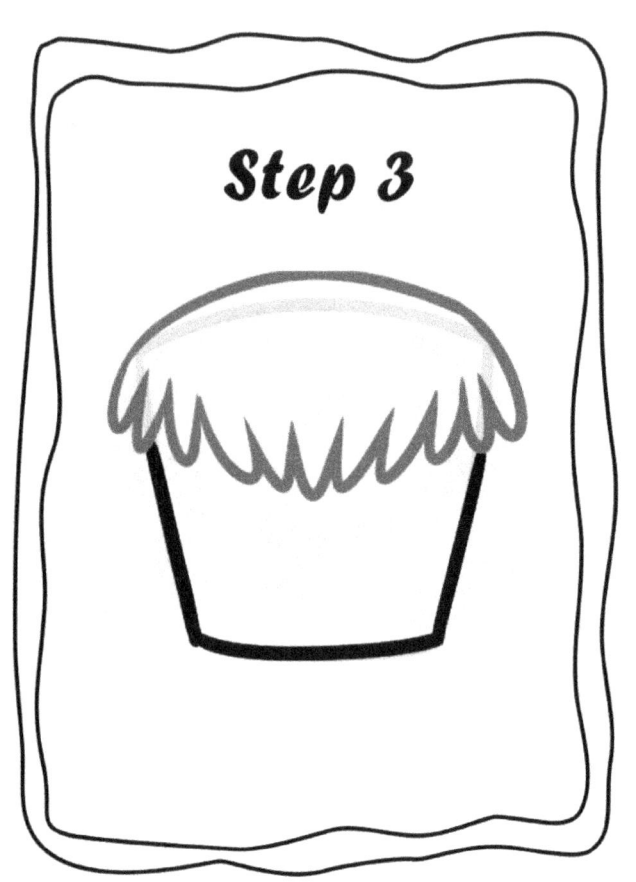

Step 4

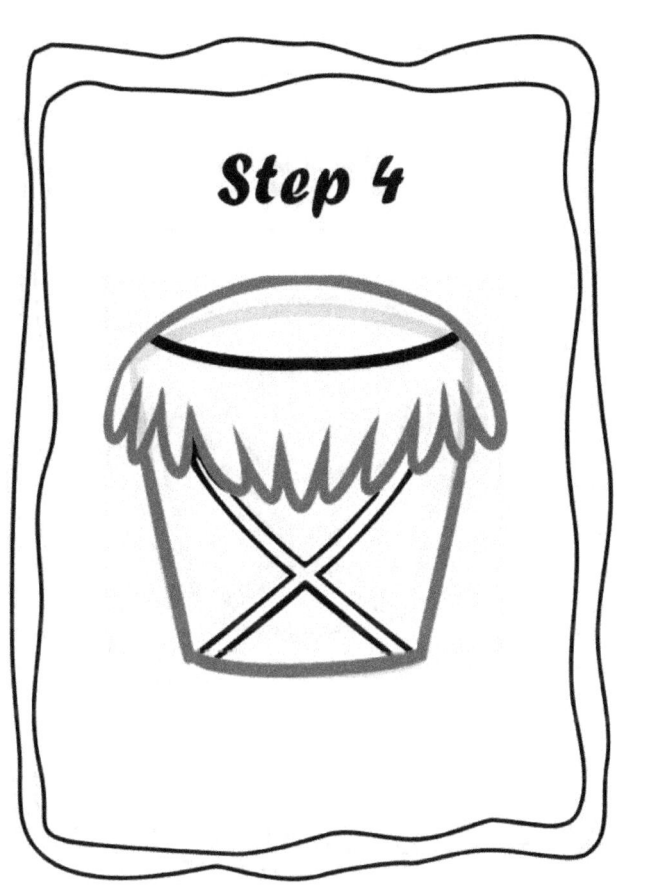

Step 5

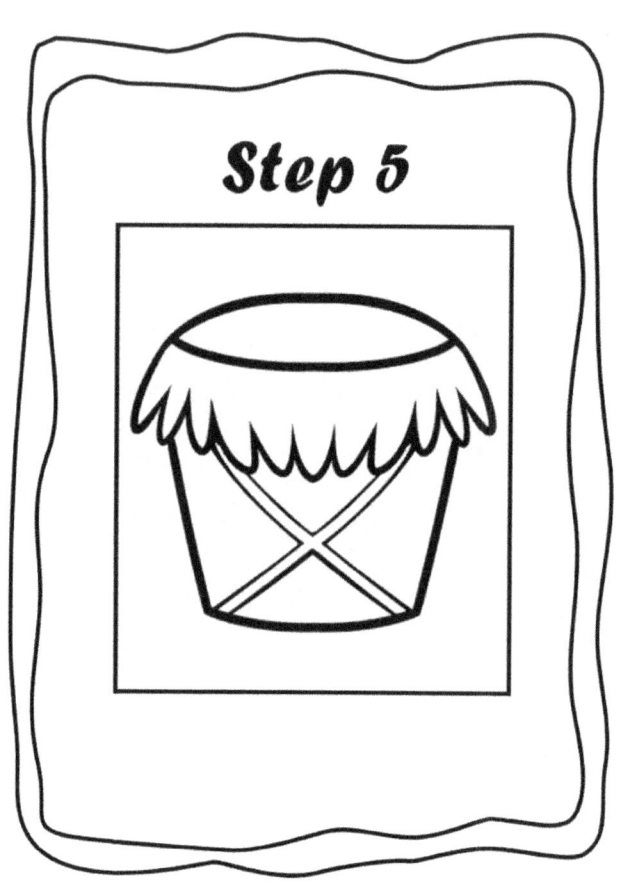

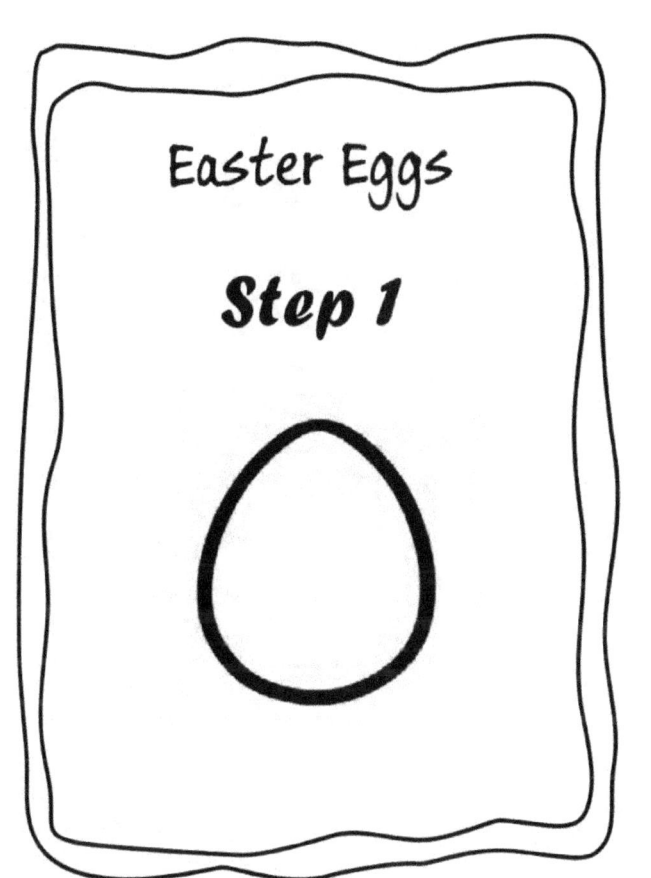

Easter Eggs

Step 1

Step 2

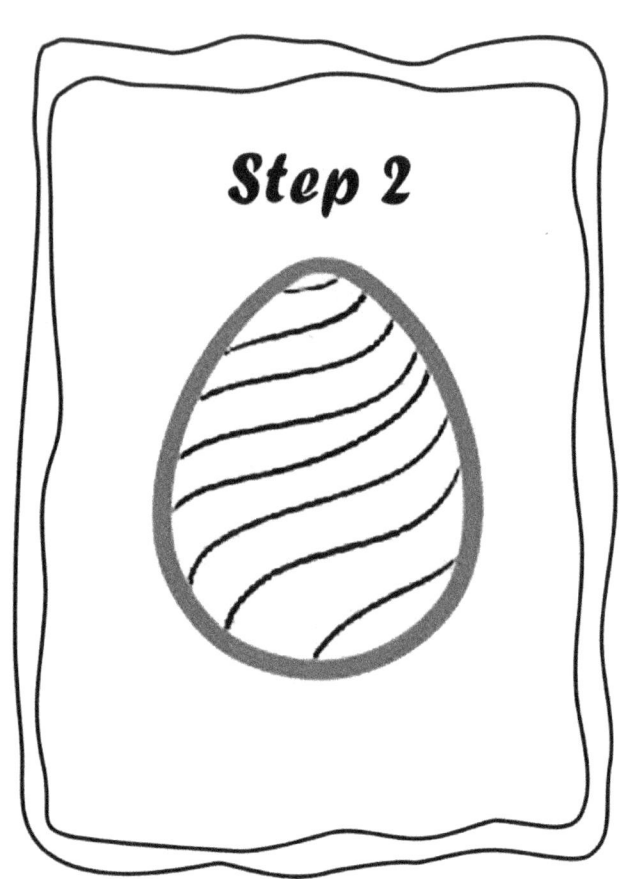

Step 3

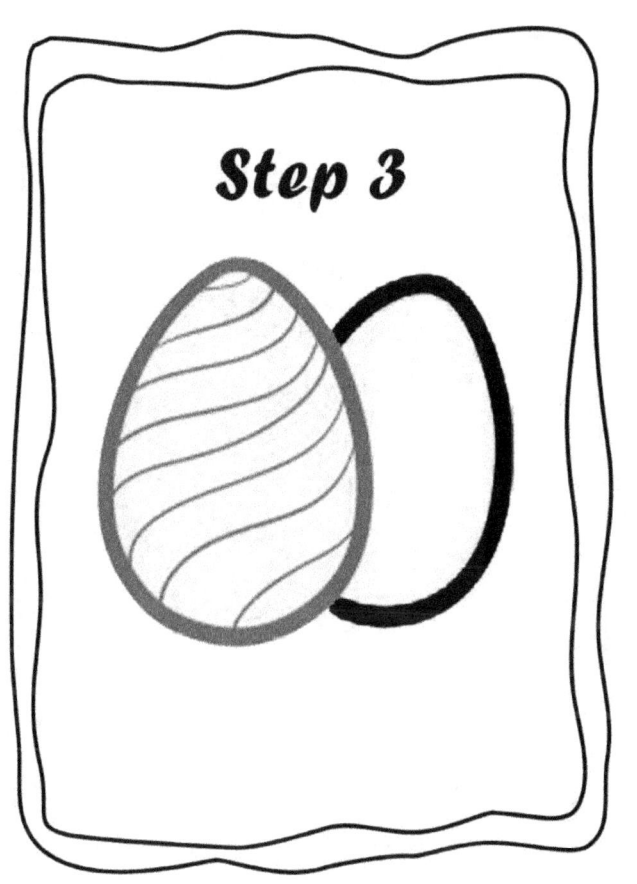

Step 4

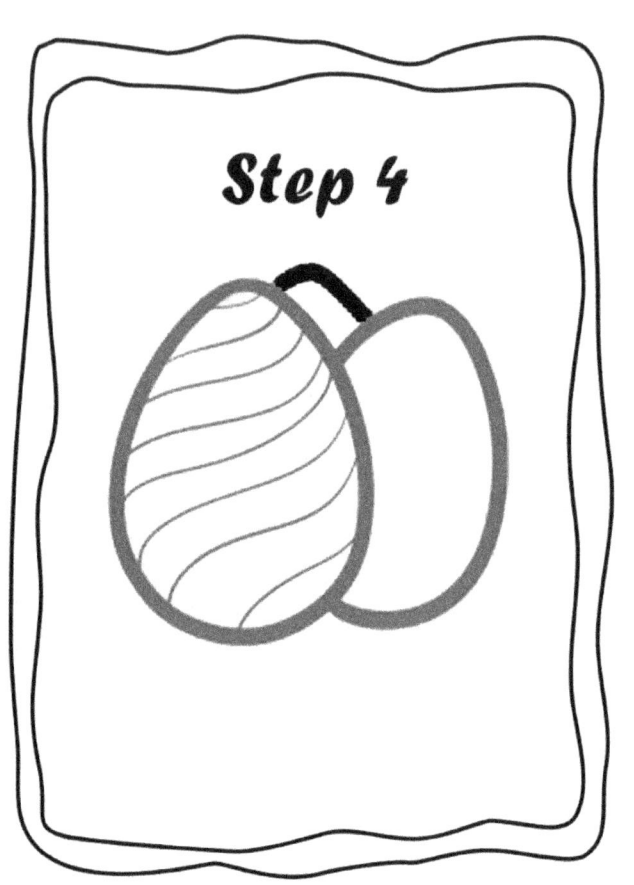

Step 5

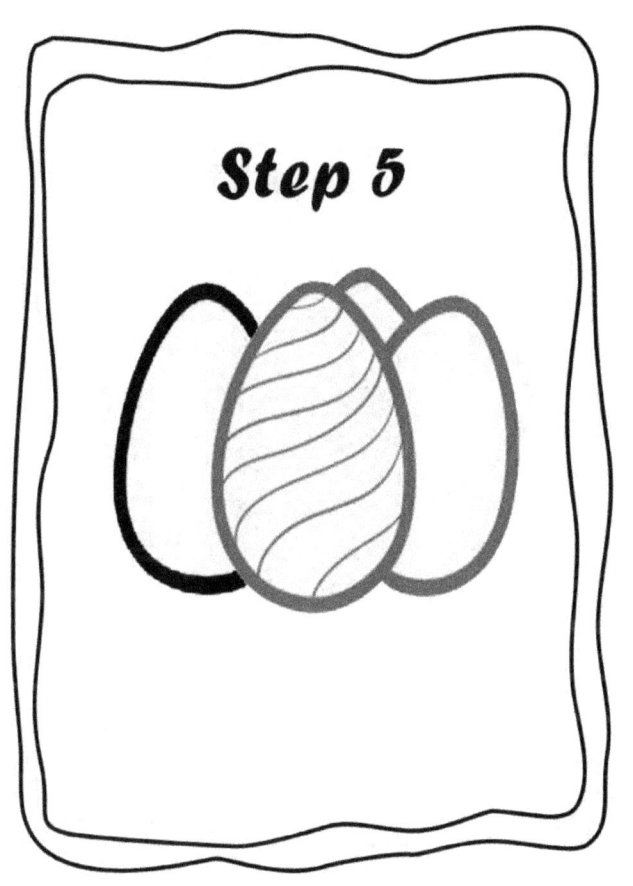

Step 6

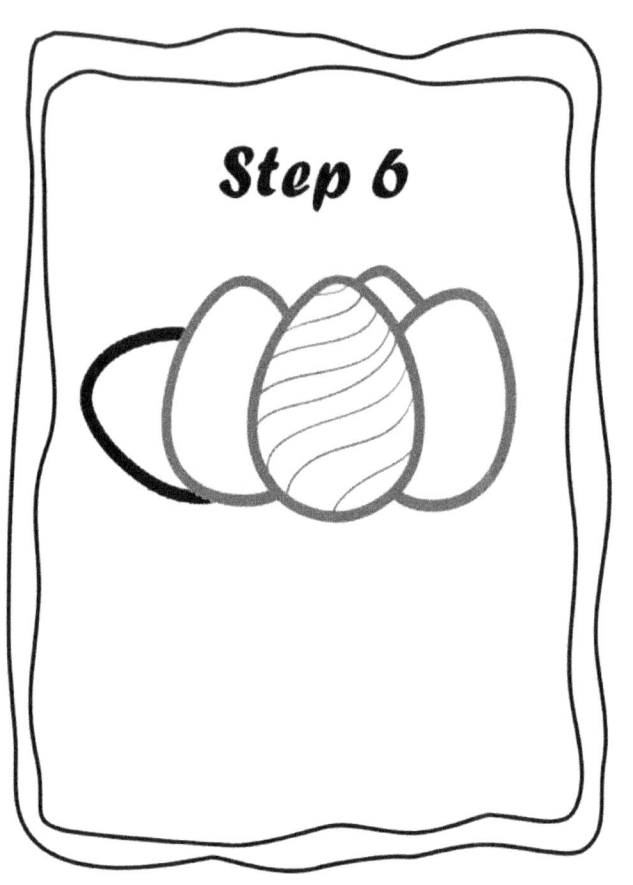

Step 7

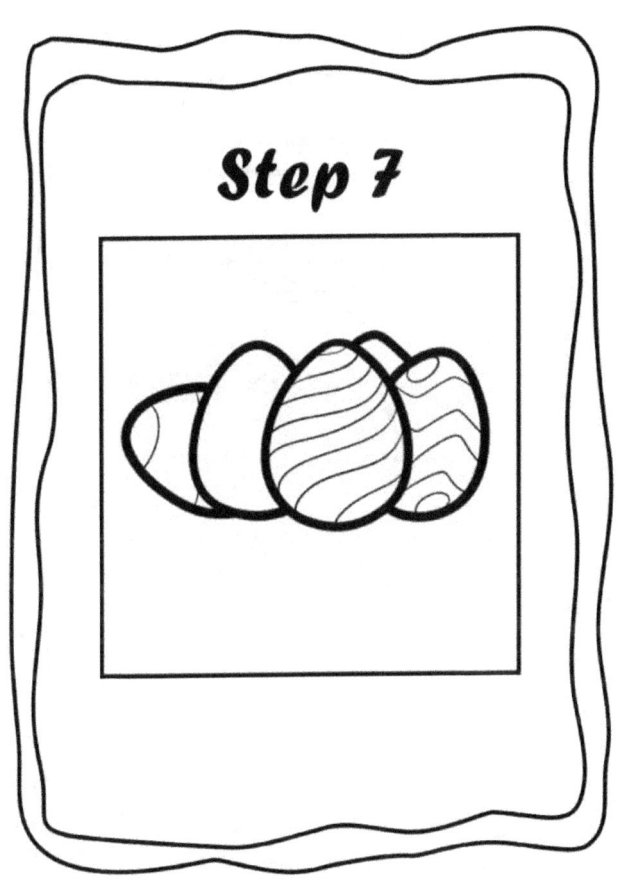

Ice Cream

Step 1

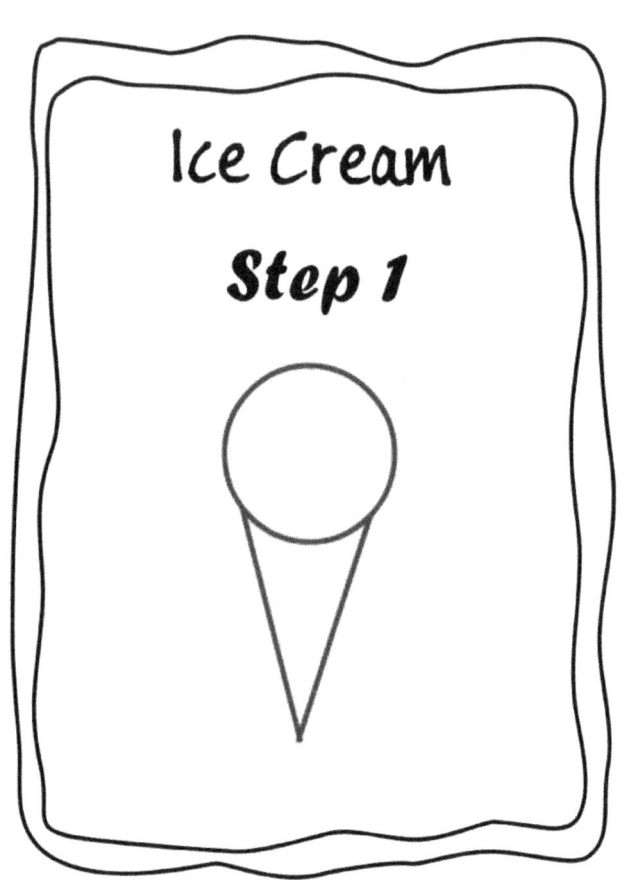

Step 2

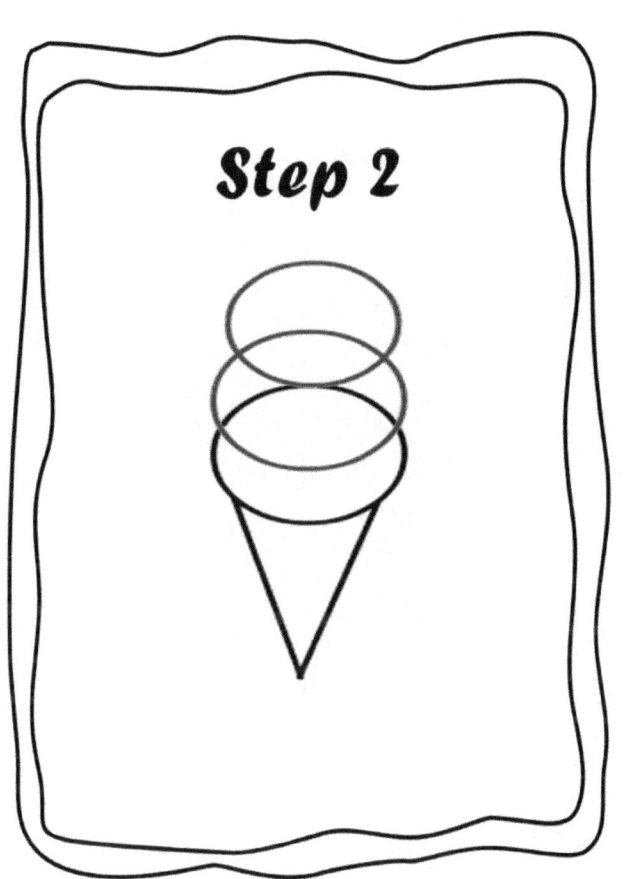

Step 3

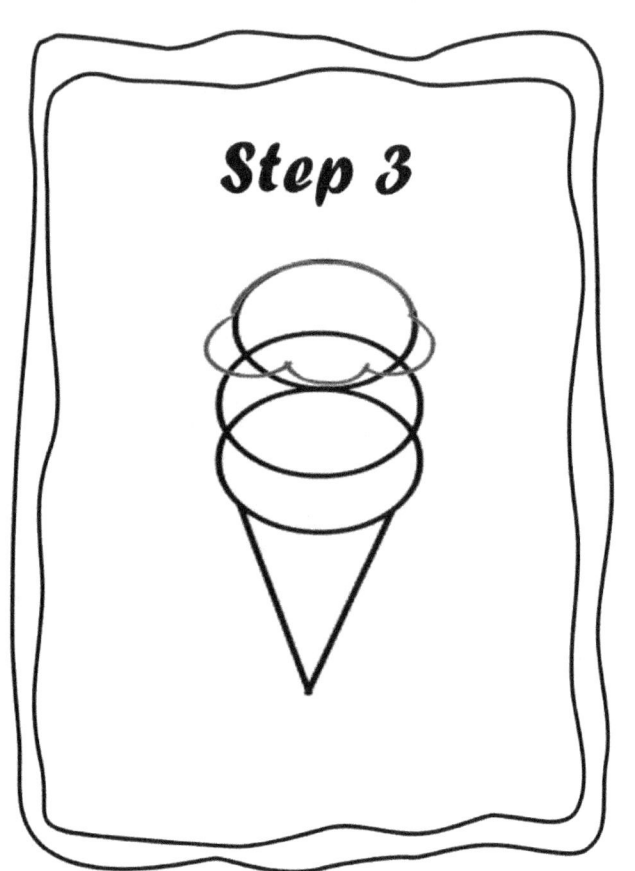

Step 4

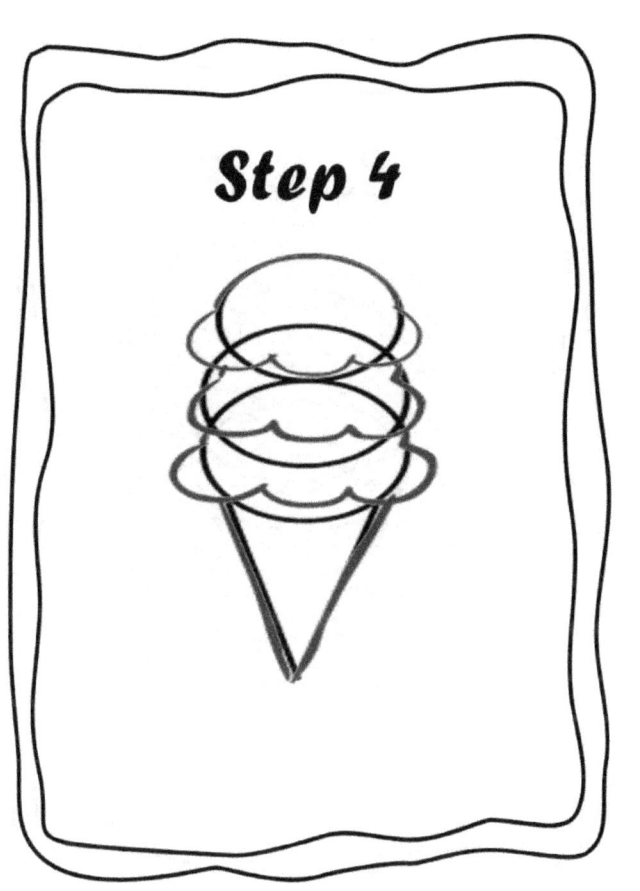

Step 5

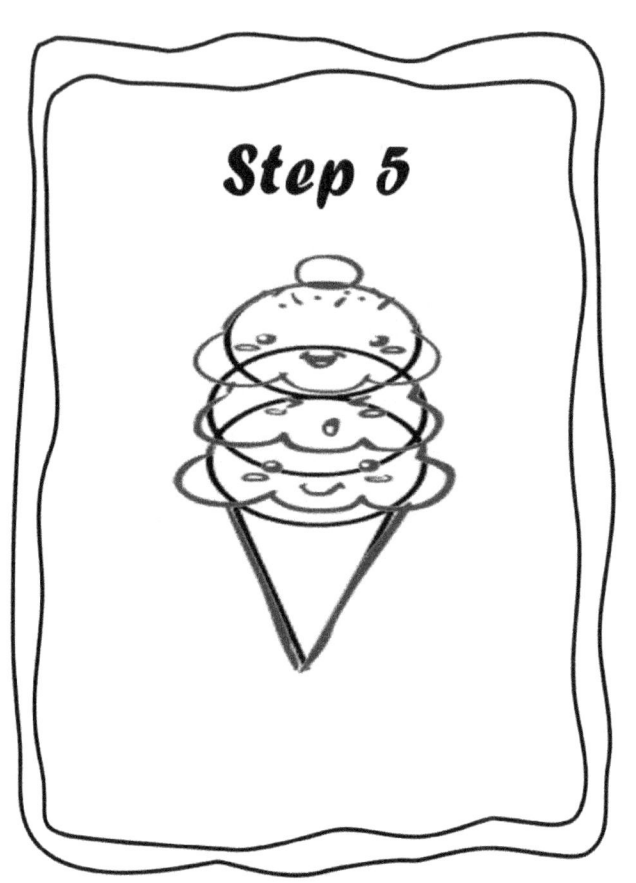

Step 6

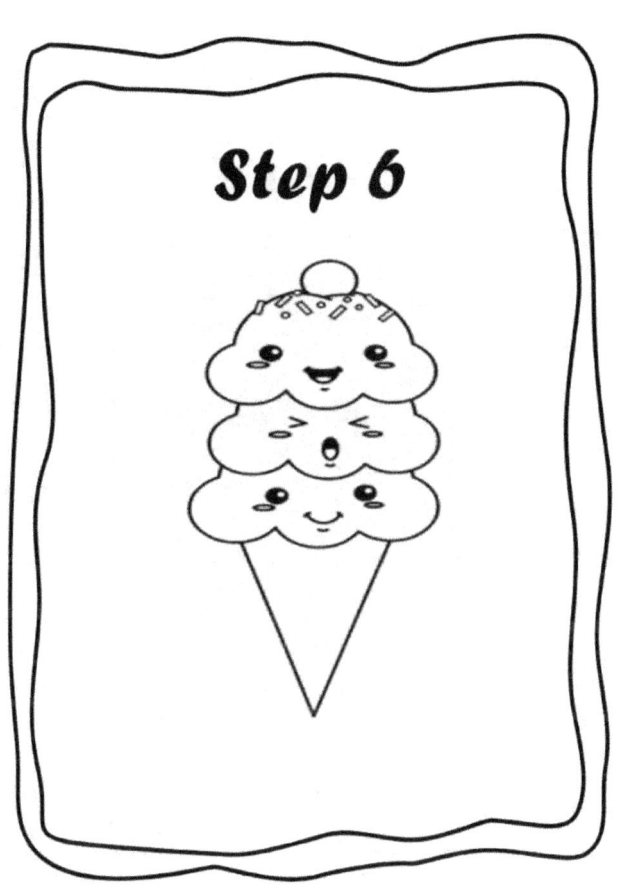

Step 7

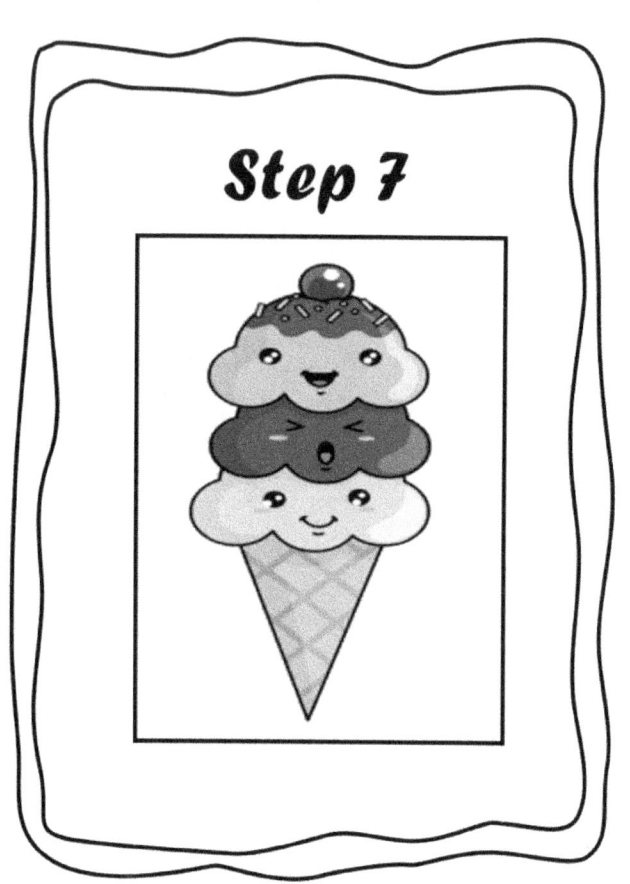

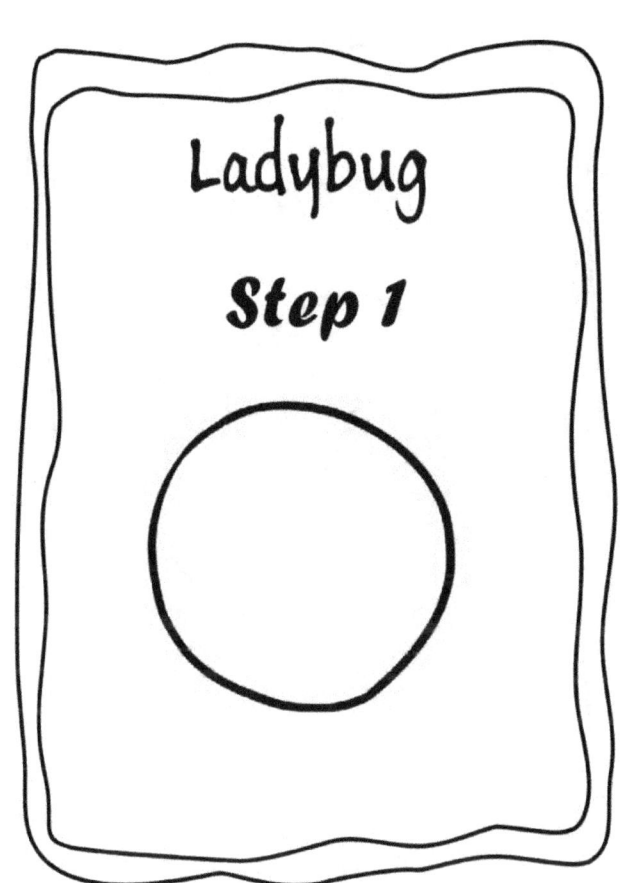

Ladybug

Step 1

Step 2

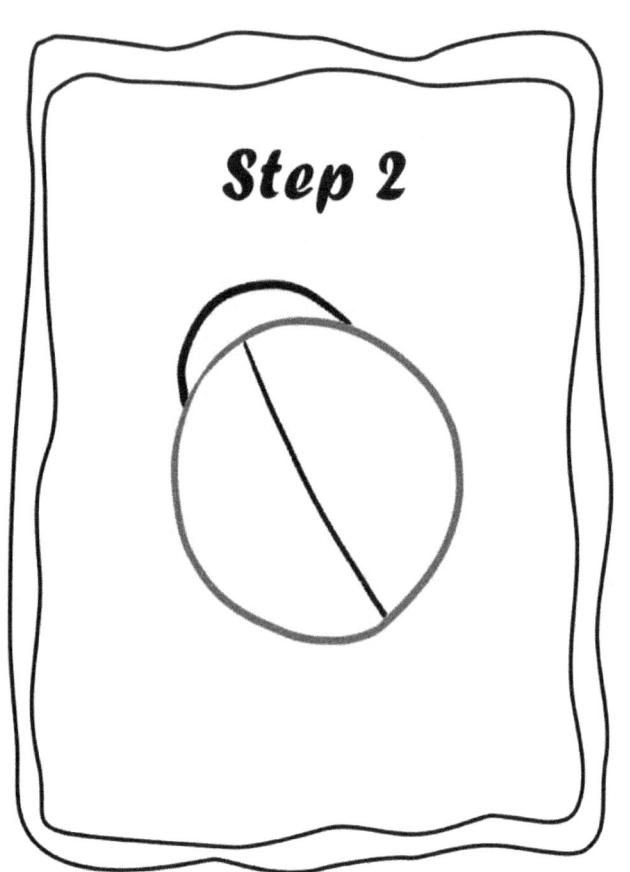

Step 3

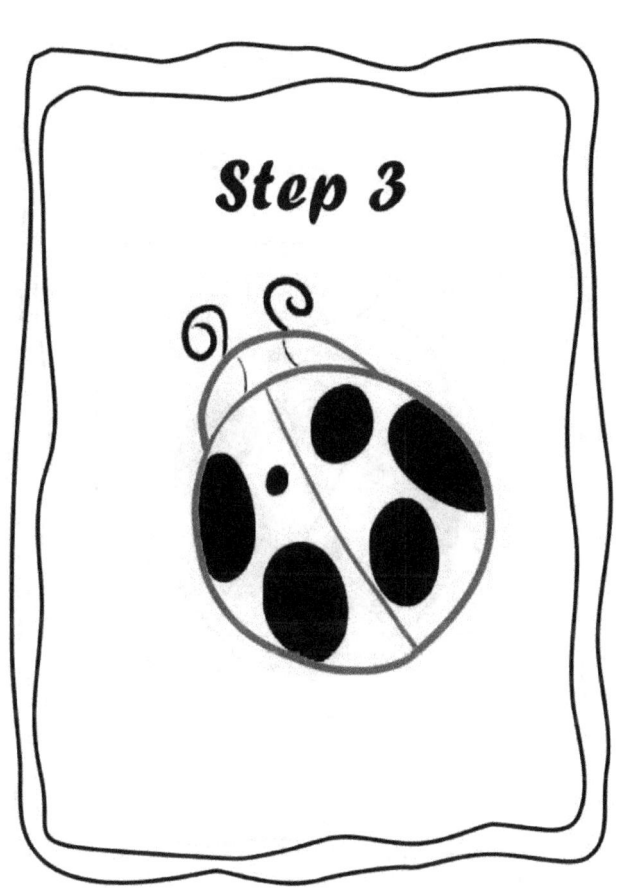

Step 4

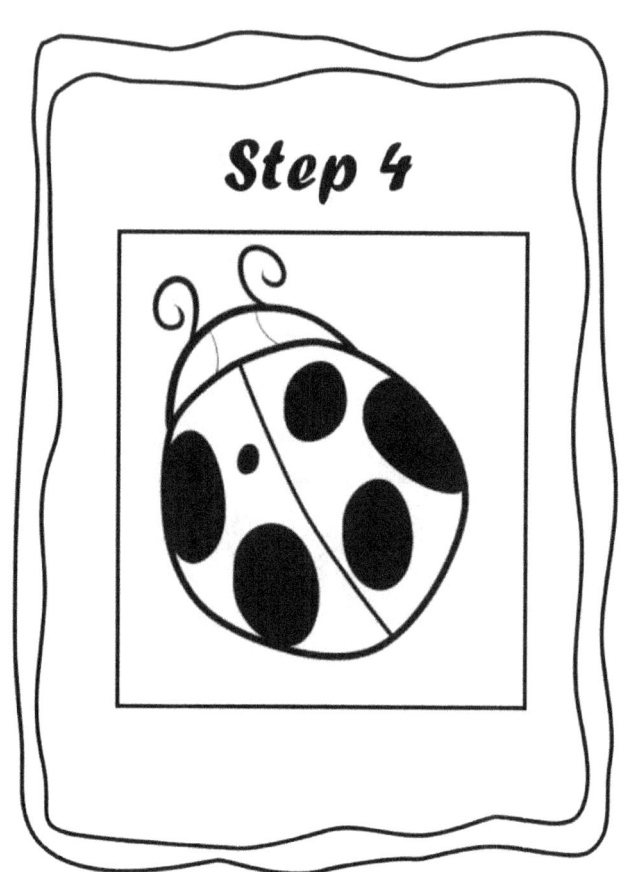

pokemon

Step 1

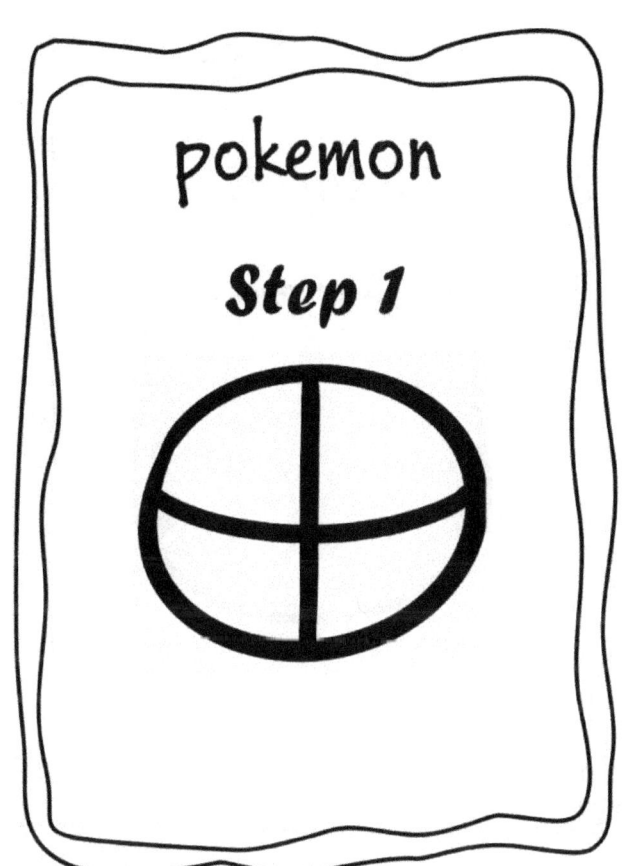

Step 2

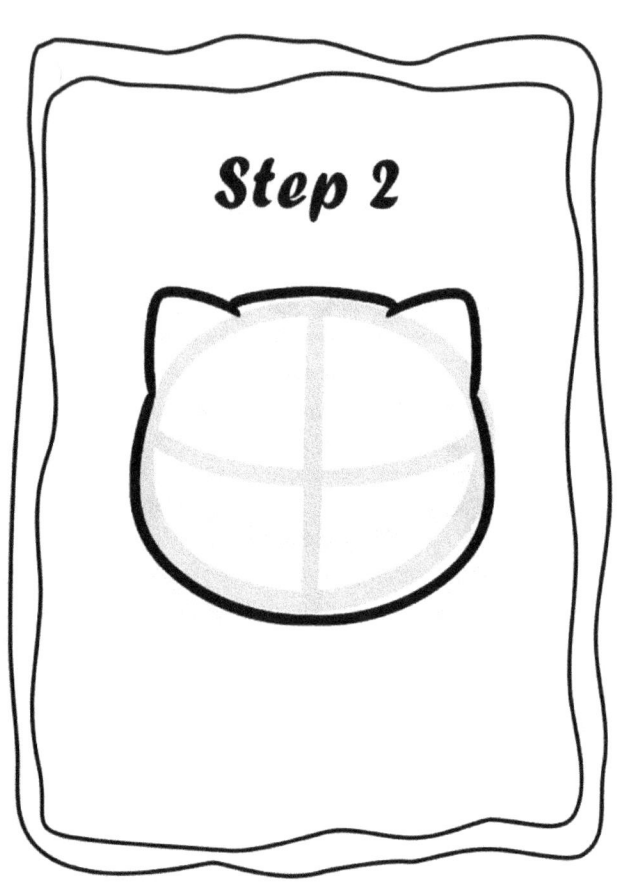

Step 3

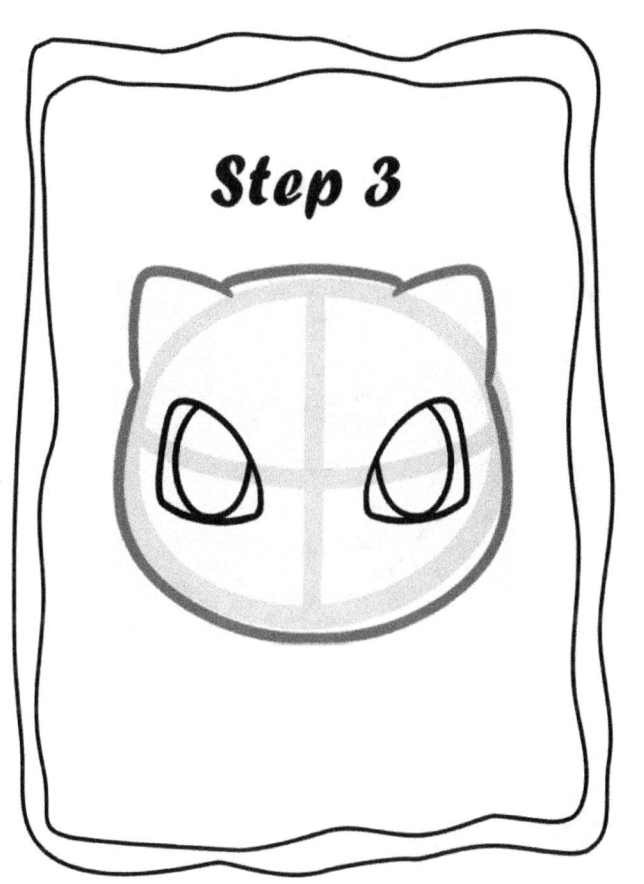

Step 4

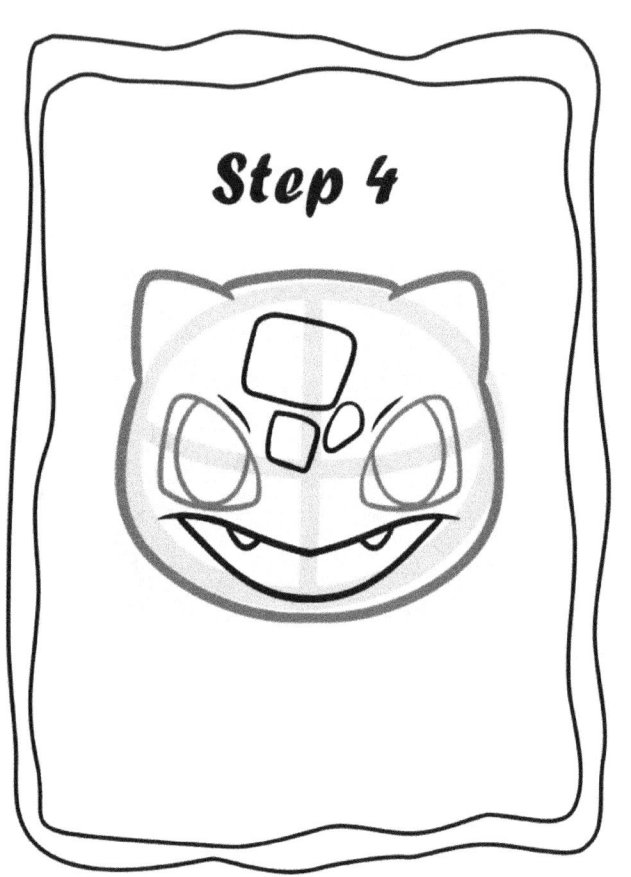

Step 5

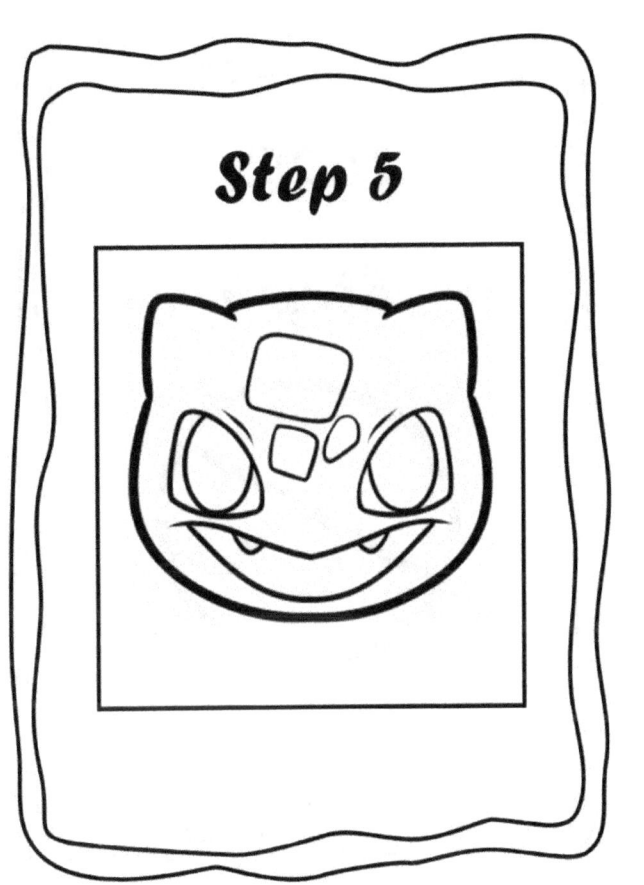

Sloth

Step 1

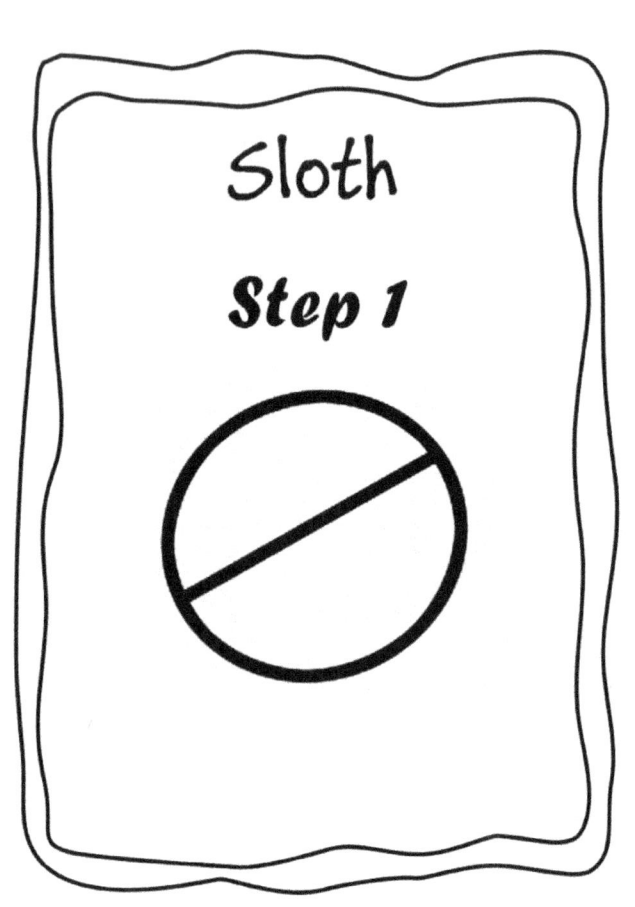

Step 2

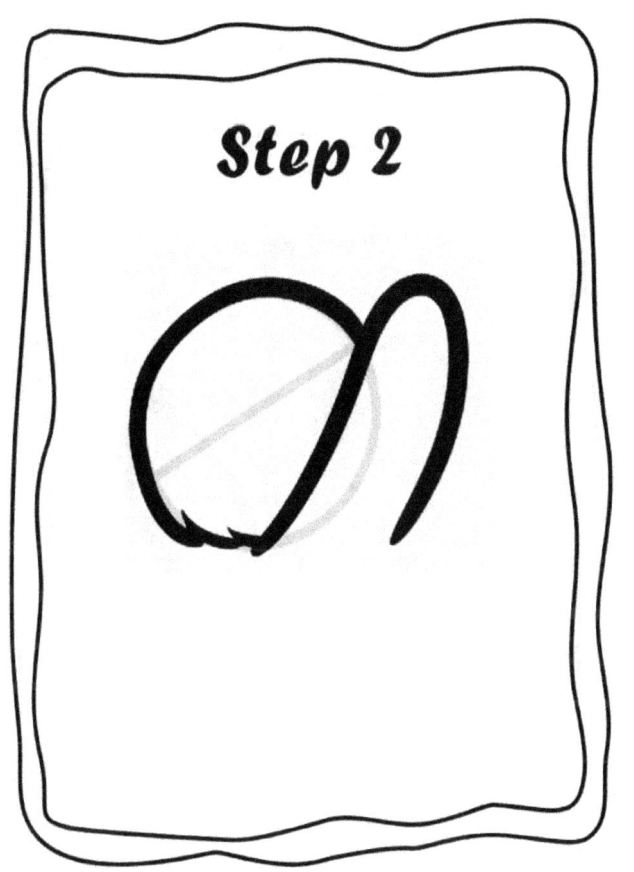

Step 3

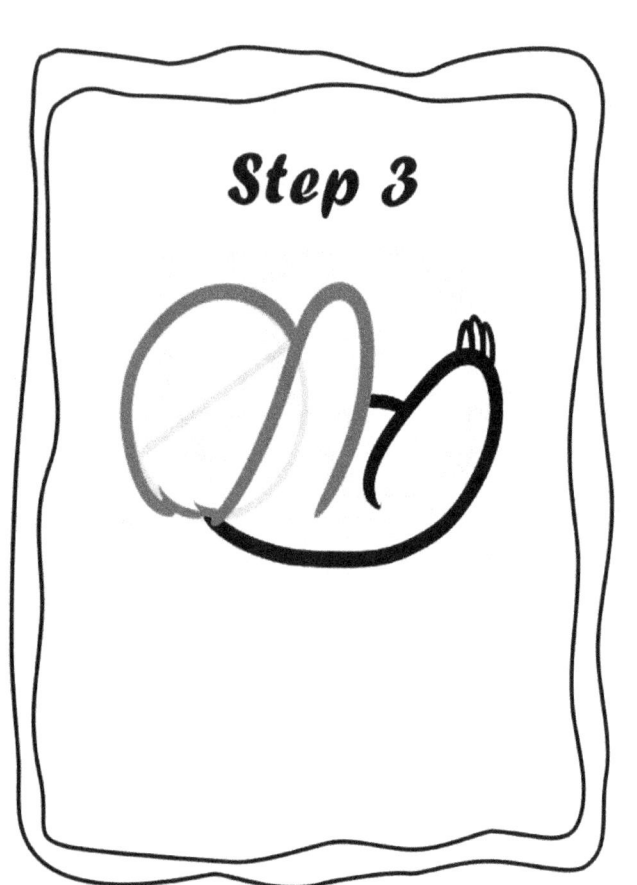

Step 4

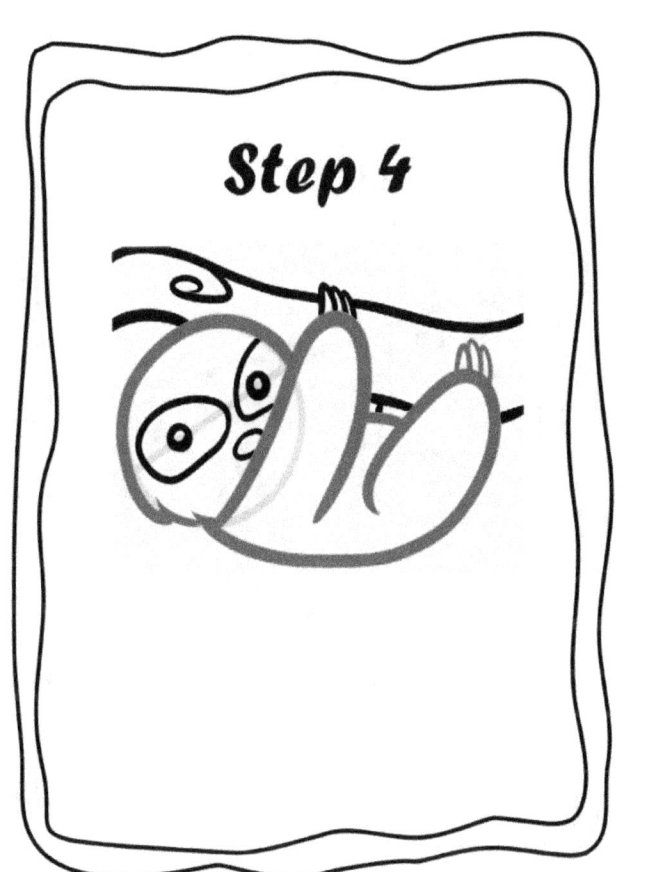

Step 5

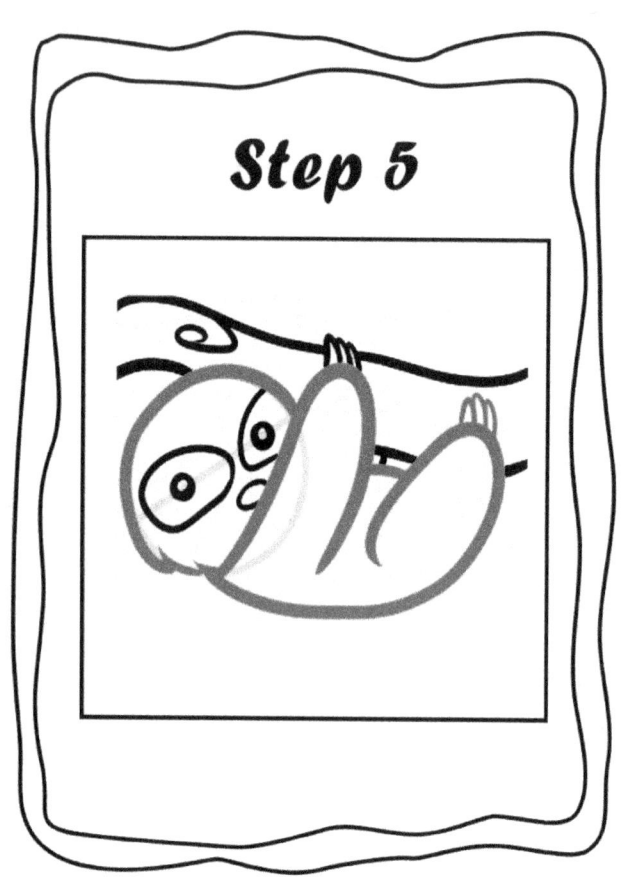

Swordfish

Step 1

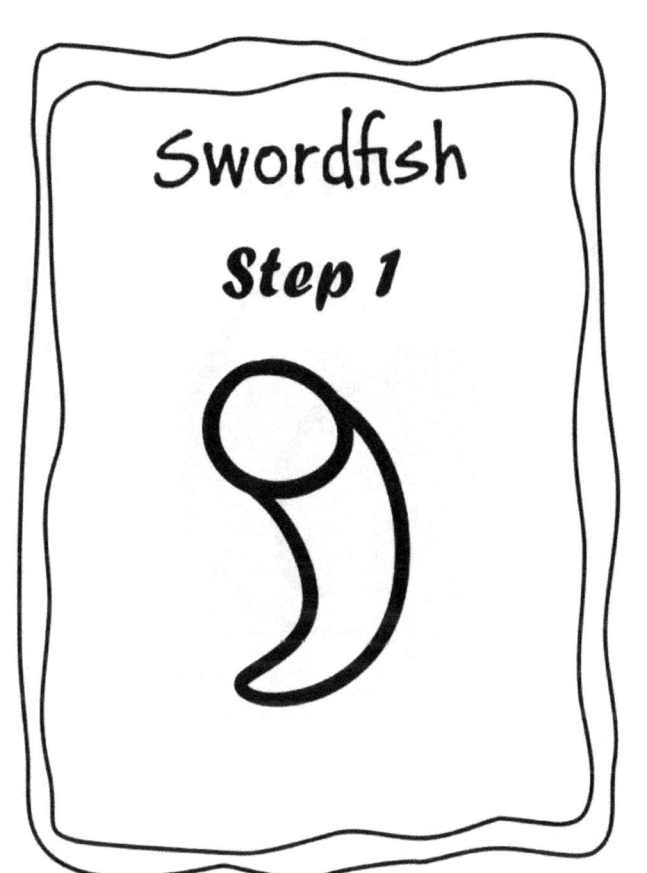

Step 2

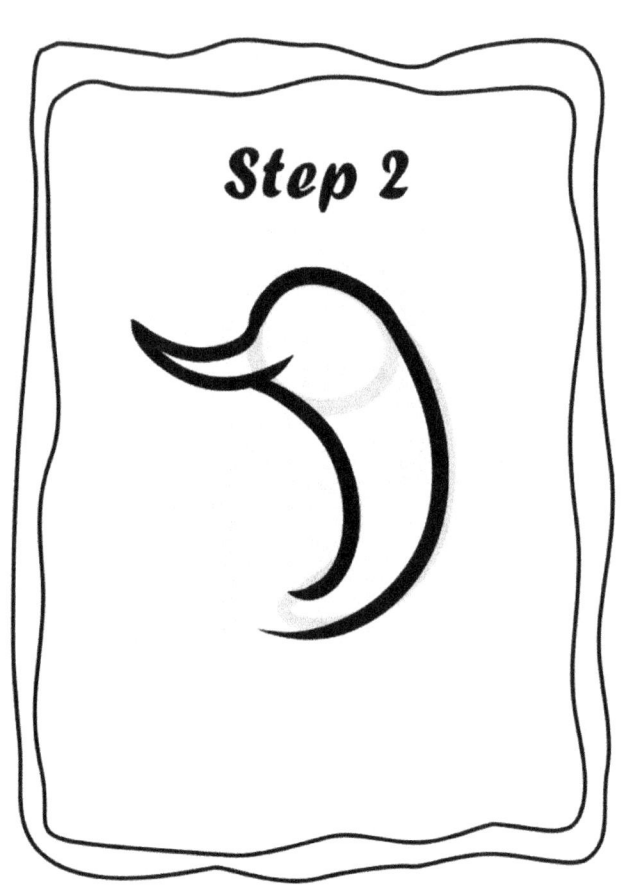

Step 3

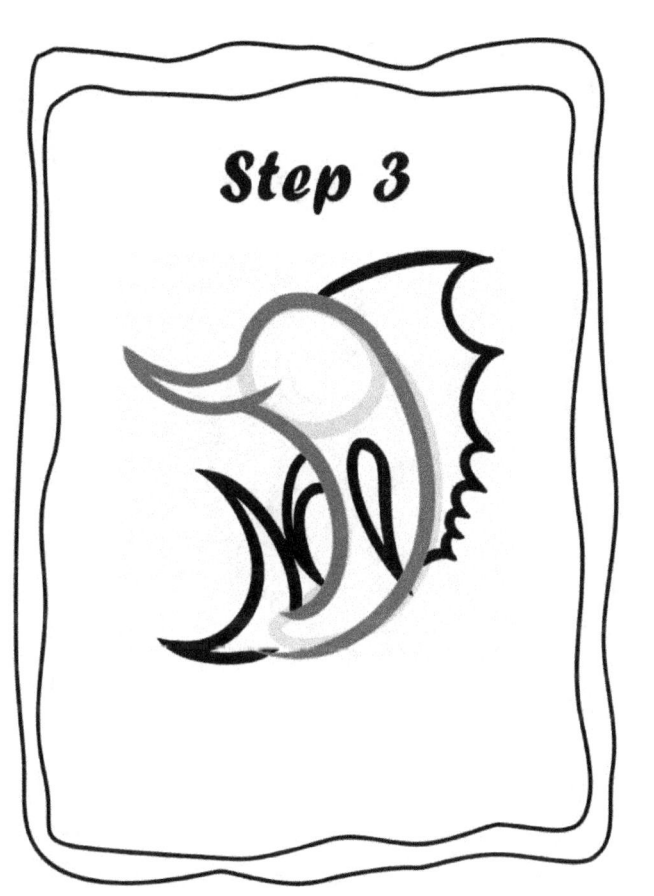

Step 4

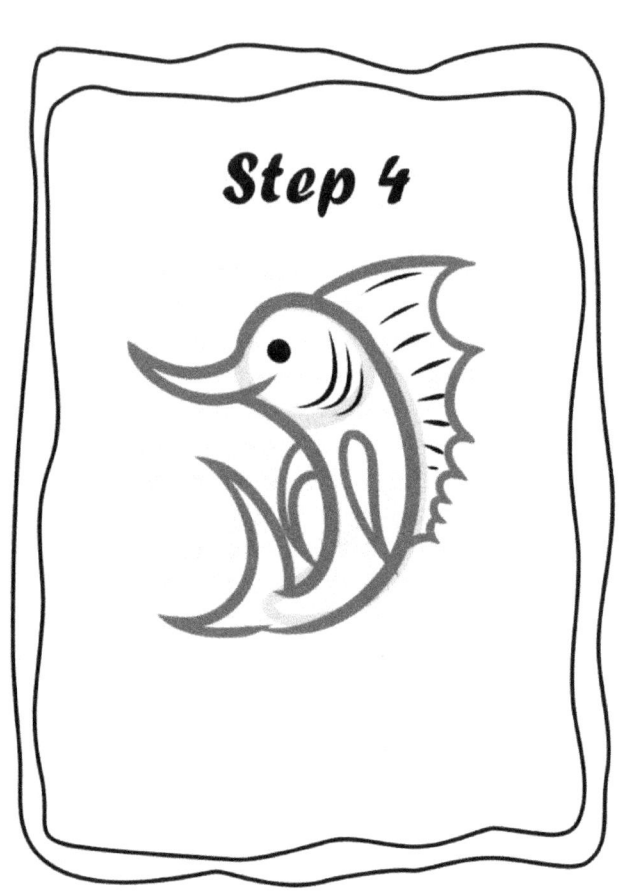

Step 5

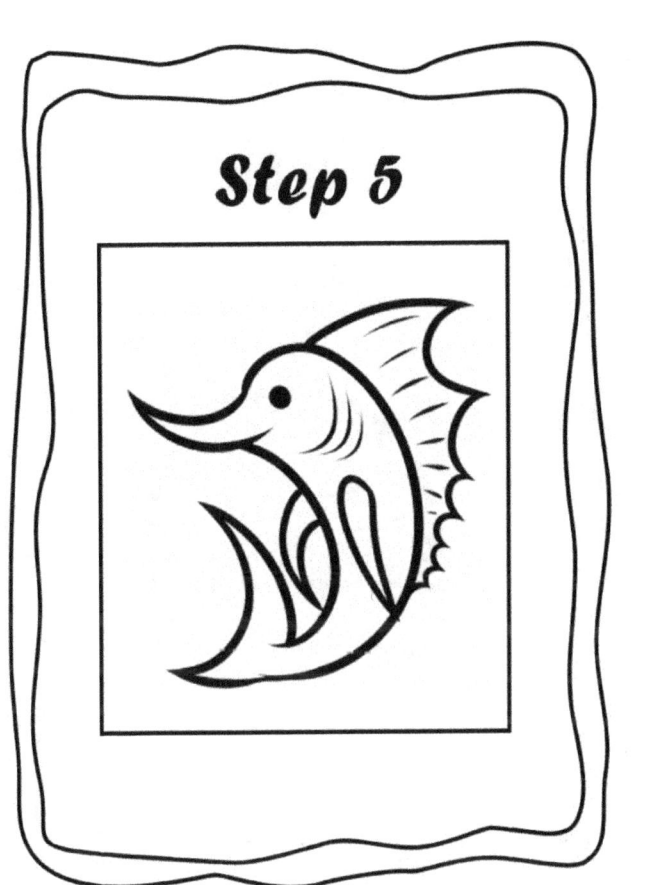

Turtle

Step 1

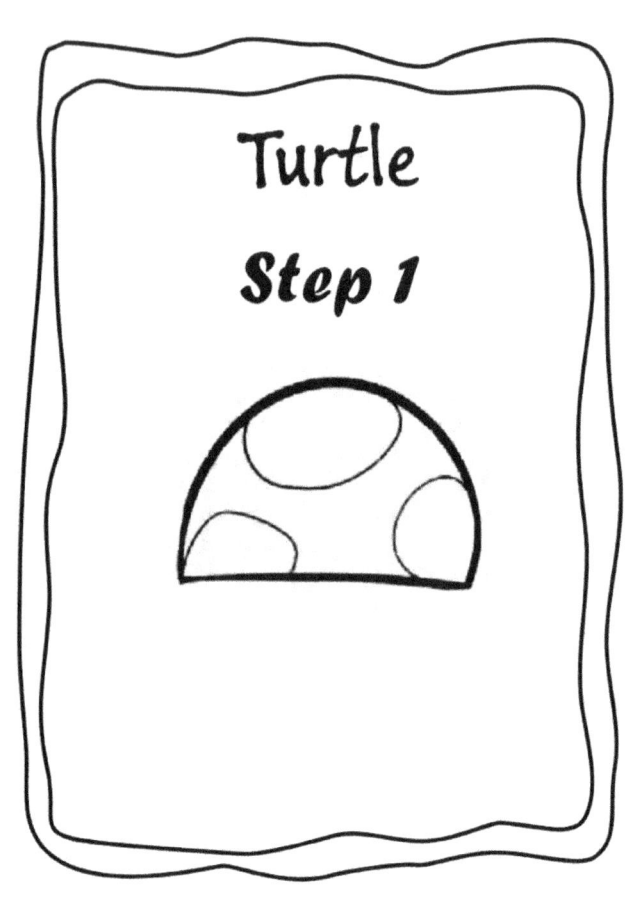

Step 2

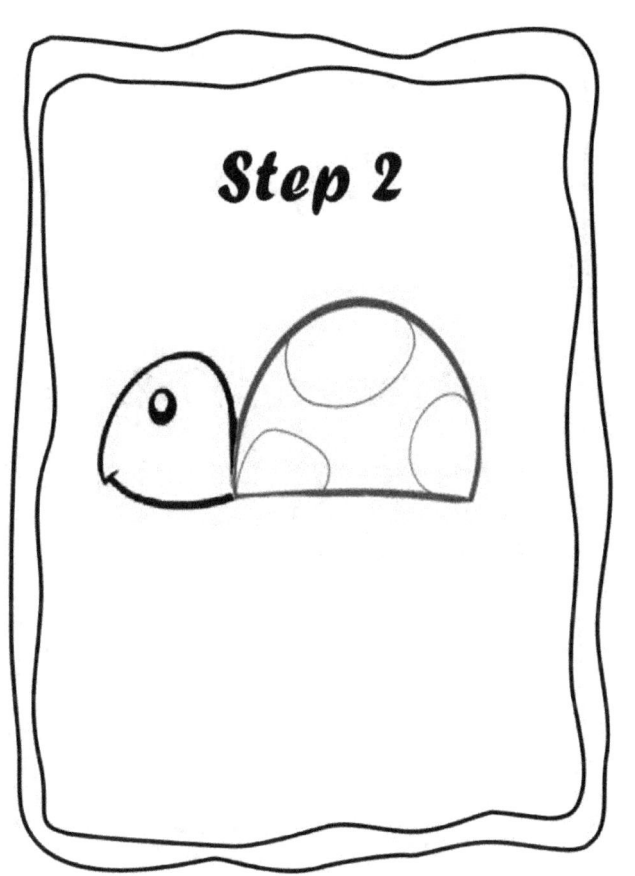

Step 3

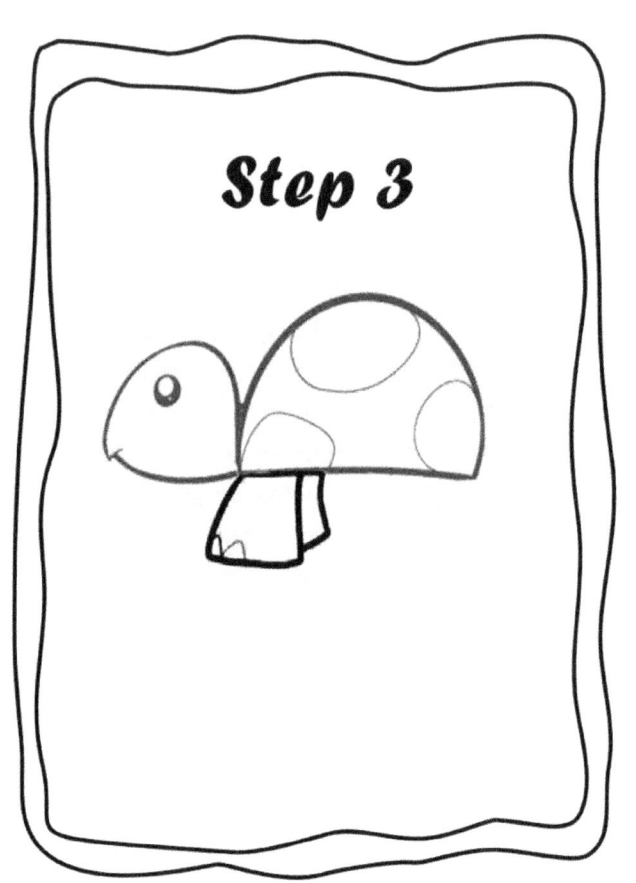

Step 4

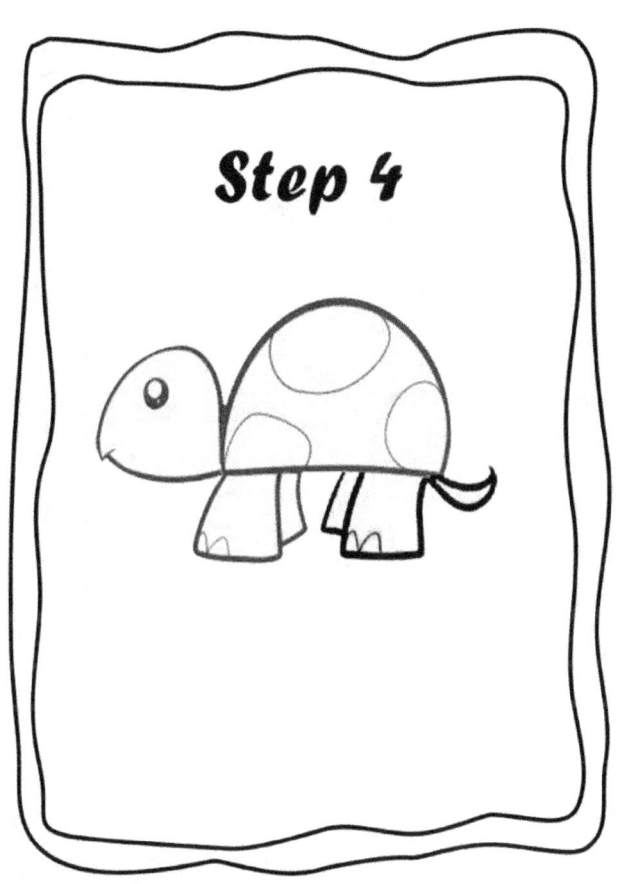

Step 5

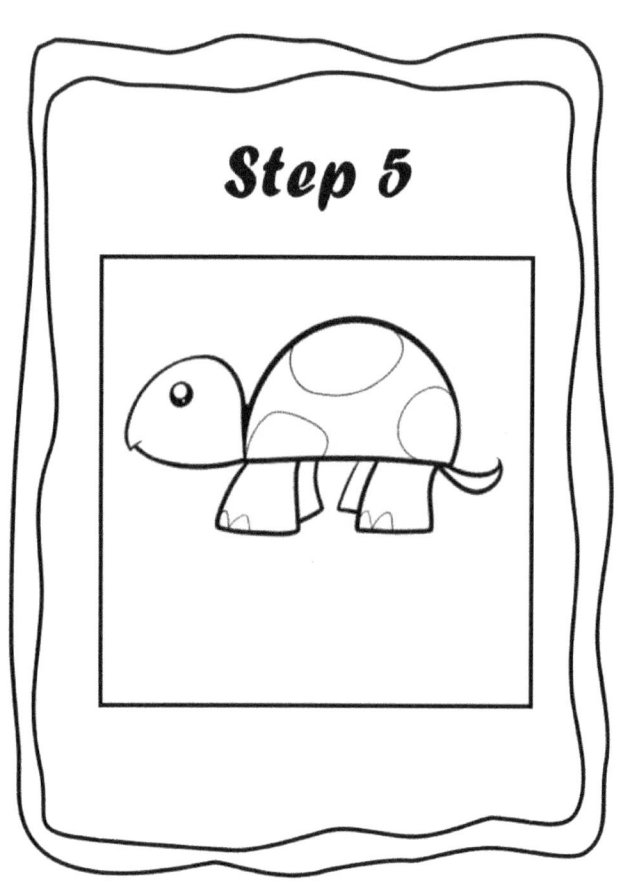

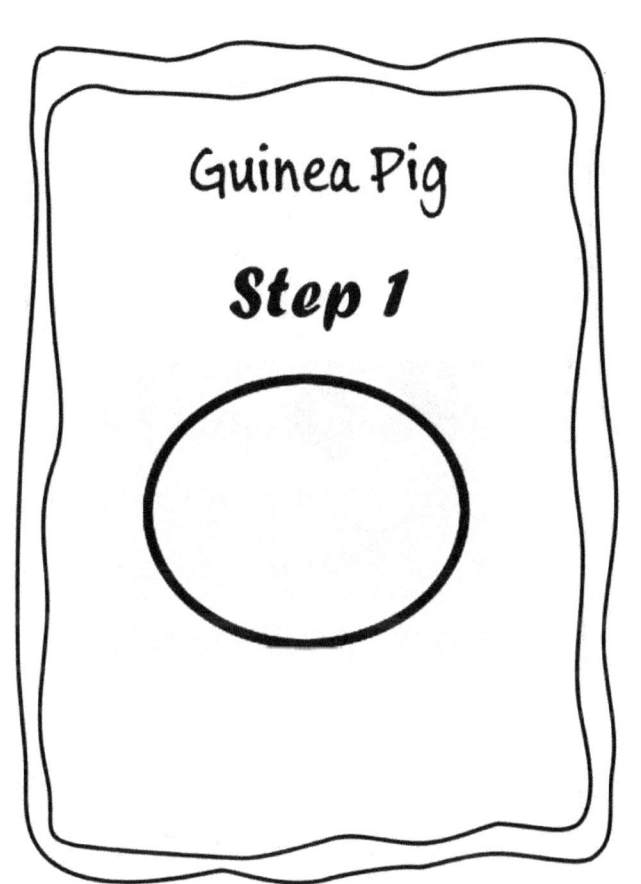

Guinea Pig

Step 1

Step 2

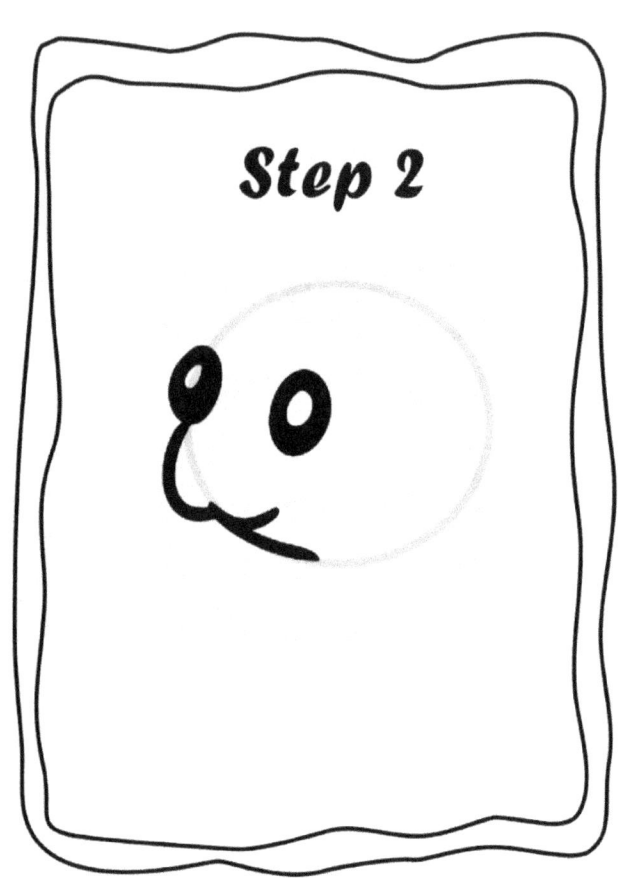

Step 3

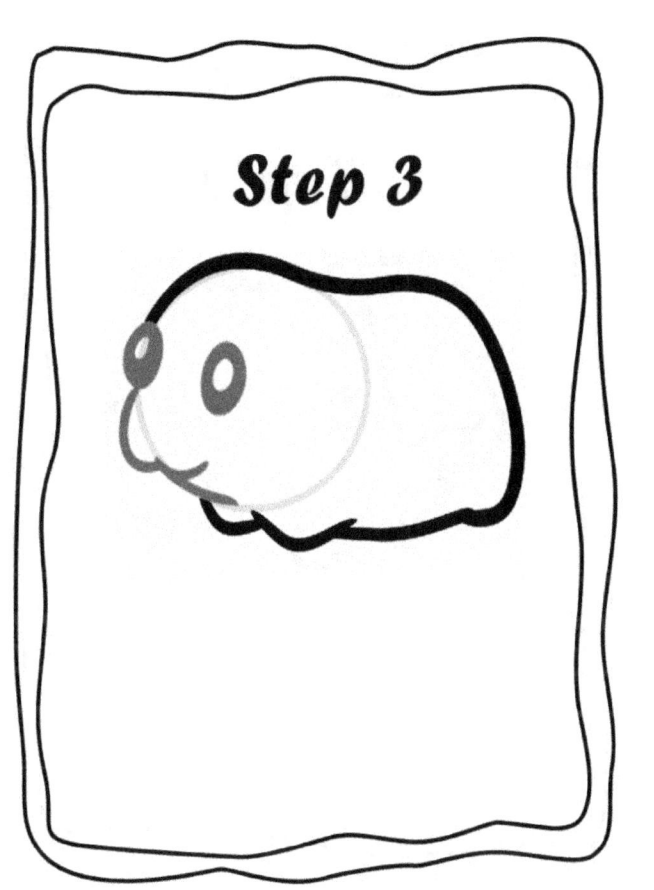

Step 4

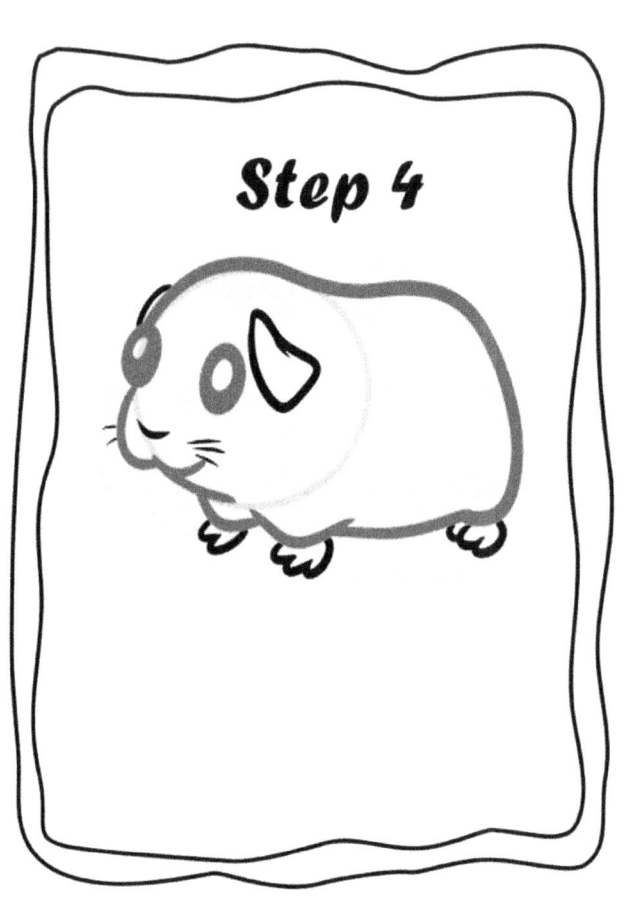

Step 5

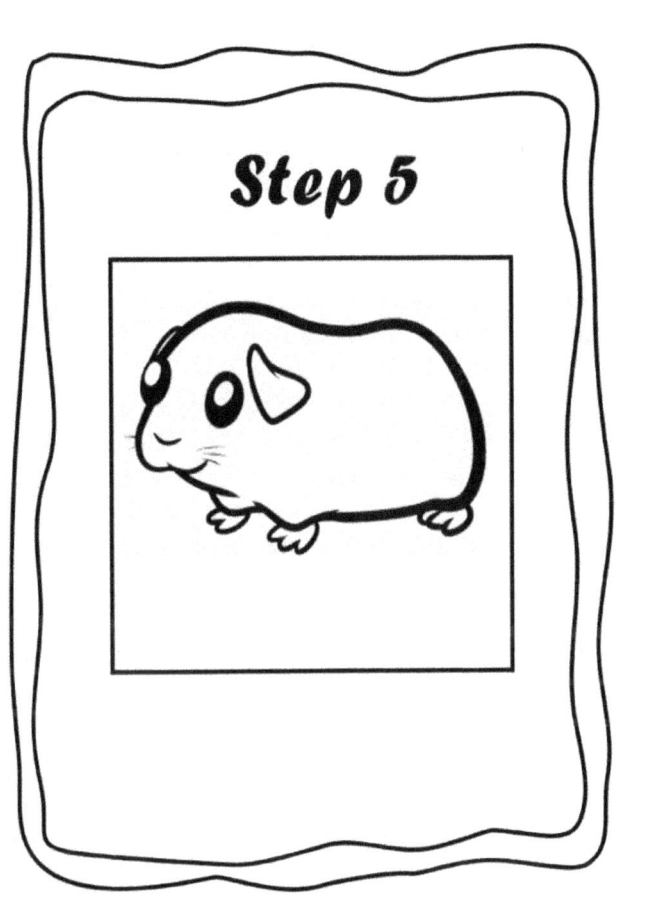

www.ingramcontent.com/pod-product-compliance
Lightning Source LLC
Chambersburg PA
CBHW070958180526
45168CB00003B/1204